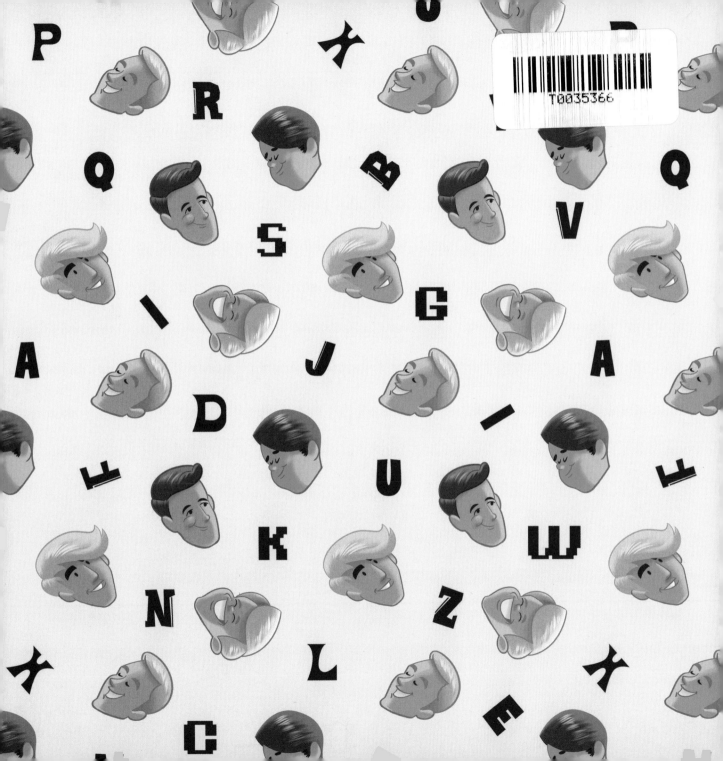
T0035366

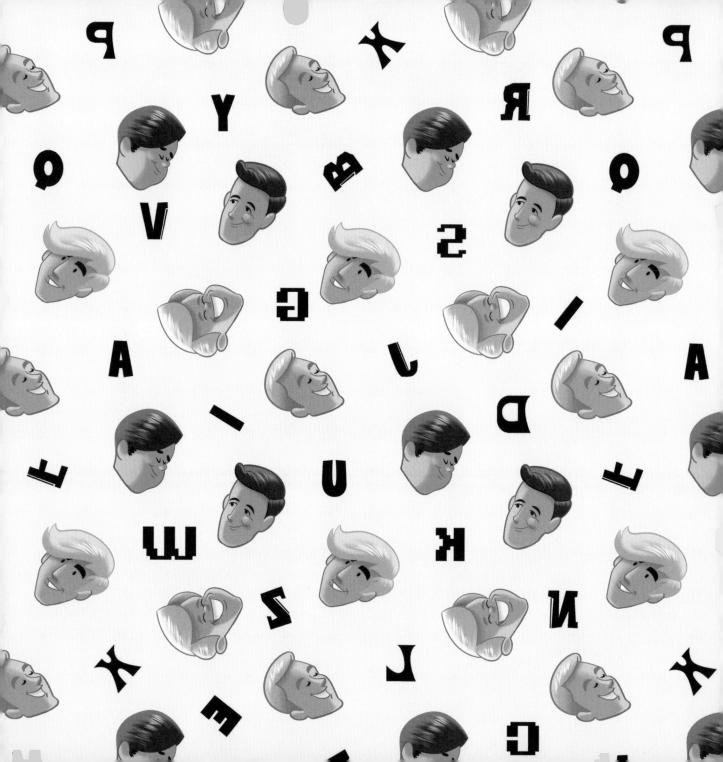

A

AL JARDINE

ALMOND TREE

AVOCADO

ANAHEIM

ARTICHOKE

FEATURED SONG:

ALL SUMMER LONG

The Beach Boys

B

BRIAN WILSON

BOAT

BURGERS

BEACH

BASS GUITAR

FEATURED SONG:
BE TRUE TO YOUR SCHOOL
The Beach Boys

C

CARL WILSON

COFFEE

CHINESE THEATRE

CELEBRITY

COYOTE

FEATURED SONG:
CALIFORNIA SAGA
The Beach Boys

D

DENNIS WILSON

DATES

DUNES

DUNE BUGGY

DRUMS

FEATURED SONG:
DANCE, DANCE, DANCE

The Beach Boys

E

EAGLE

EXERCISE

EARTHQUAKE

ELECTRIC CAR

EUREKA

FEATURED SONG:

EVERYONE'S IN LOVE WITH YOU

The Beach Boys

F

FRESNO

FRUIT

FISHERMAN'S WHARF

FRIENDS

CALIFORNIA REPUBLIC

FLAG

FEATURED SONG:
FUN, FUN, FUN

The Beach Boys

G

GOLDEN GATE
BRIDGE

GRIFFITH
OBSERVATORY

GRIZZLY BEAR

GRAPES

GETTY
MUSEUM

FEATURED SONG:

GOOD TO MY BABY

The Beach Boys

H

HOT ROD

HOLLYWOOD

HARMONY

HAWTHORNE

HIGHWAY

FEATURED SONG:
HONKIN' DOWN THE HIGHWAY
The Beach Boys

I

ISLAND

ILLUSTRATION

INSTRUMENT

INSECT

ICE CREAM

FEATURED SONG:

I GET AROUND

The Beach Boys

J

JADE

JACKRABBIT

JOSHUA TREE
NATIONAL PARK

JELLYFISH

JUICE

FEATURED SONG:
JOHNNY CARSON
The Beach Boys

K

KALE

KAYAK

KELP FOREST

KLAMATH MOUNTAINS

KILLIFISH

FEATURED SONG:
KEEPIN' THE SUMMER ALIVE
The Beach Boys

L

LOBSTER

LIFEGUARD

LOS ANGELES

LITTLE DEUCE COUPE

LILAC

FEATURED SONG:
LITTLE OLD LADY FROM PASADENA

The Beach Boys

M

MIKE LOVE

MICROPHONE

MOUNTAIN LION

MANSION

MOJAVE DESERT

FEATURED SONG:
THE MAN WITH ALL THE TOYS

The Beach Boys

N

NATURE

NEST

NAPA VALLEY

NUTRIA

NATIONAL PARK

FEATURED SONG:
NOBLE SURFER
The Beach Boys

O

ORANGE

OYSTER

OCEAN

ORCA

OTTER

FEATURED SONG:
OUR TEAM

The Beach Boys

P

PEACH

PET

PALM SPRINGS

POPPIES

PALM TREES

FEATURED SONG:
PLEASE LET ME WONDER
The Beach Boys

Q

QUINOA

QUINTET

QUAIL

QUILT

QUEEN

QUESTION: WHAT IS YOUR FAVORITE BEACH BOYS SONG?

The Beach Boys

R

RACCOON

RATTLESNAKE

RECORD

THE RONETTES

RODEO DRIVE

ROLLERSKATING CHILD

FEATURED SONG:
ROCKING SURFER
The Beach Boys

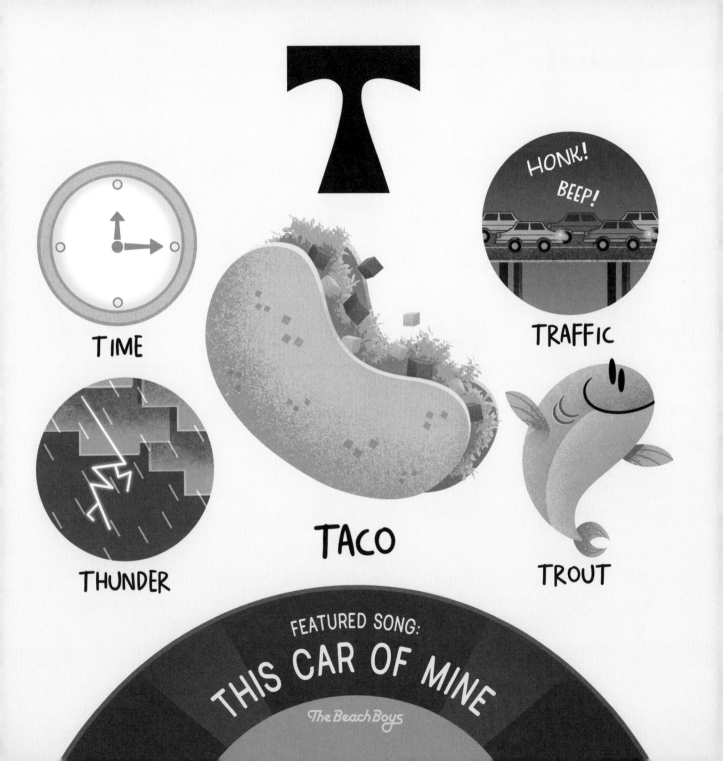

U

USS MIDWAY

UNIFORM

UPPER LAKE

UMBRELLA

UKULELE

FUN, FUN, FACT: A UKULELE WAS USED ON THE "PET SOUNDS" ALBUM

The Beach Boys

V

VACATION

VOLLEYBALL

VULTURE

VENICE BEACH

VEGETABLES

FEATURED SONG:
VEGETABLES

The Beach Boys

W

WOODLAND HILLS

WALNUTS

WHISTLING

WILD HONEY

WATERMELON

FEATURED SONG:
WIND CHIMES
The Beach Boys

X

X MARKS THE SPOT

XYLOPHONE

XERISCAPING
WOW! A TOUGH WORD, CAN YOU REPEAT IT WITH YOUR PARENTS?

FUN, FUN, FACT: A XYLOPHONE WAS USED IN THE SONG "ALL SUMMER LONG"

The Beach Boys

Y

YOGA

YARROW

YOSEMITE

YELLOWFIN TUNA

YUMA BAT

FEATURED SONG:
YOU'RE SO GOOD TO ME
The Beach Boys

Z

ZUCCHINI

ZEBU

ZEBRA

ZOO

ZINNIAS

I'M SLEEPY! WHY DON'T WE CATCH SOME Z'S?

The Beach Boys

Created at

Fantoons Animation Studios

ART DIRECTION BY:
DAVID CALCANO

WRITTEN BY:
DAVID CALCANO AND LINDSAY LEE

ILLUSTRATIONS BY:
LINDSAY LEE AND ALBERTO BELANDRIA

LETTERING BY:
EDUARDO BRAUN

PRODUCED BY:
LINDA OTERO AND DIANA VILLENA

BOOK LAYOUT DESIGN BY:
BRETT BURNER

GRAPHIC DESIGN BY:
ALBERTO BELANDRIA AND CATHERIN CHINEA

EDITS BY:
STEVE COLLE

SALES: INFO@FANTOONS.TV
HTTPS://FANTOONS.TV/
HTTPS://THEBEACHBOYS.COM

NO PART OF THIS PUBLICATION MAY BE REPRODUCED, DISTRIBUTED OR
TRANSMITTED IN ANY FORM OR BY ANY MEANS, ELECTRONIC, MECHANICAL,
PHOTOCOPYING OR OTHERWISE, WITHOUT PRIOR PERMISSION OF THE
AUTHOR.

ALL CHARACTER DESIGNS © 2023 FANTOONS AND ICONIC BROTHERS IP LLC.
THE BEACH BOYS PRESENT: THE ABC'S OF CALIFORNIA IS PRODUCED BY
FANTOONS, WOODLAND HILLS, CA
FANTOONS.TV/BOOKS/

© 2023 ICONIC BROTHERS IP LLC. THE BEACH BOYS ™ UNDER LICENSE TO
ICONIC BROTHERS IP LLC.

PRINTED IN CHINA
ISBN:978-1970047264

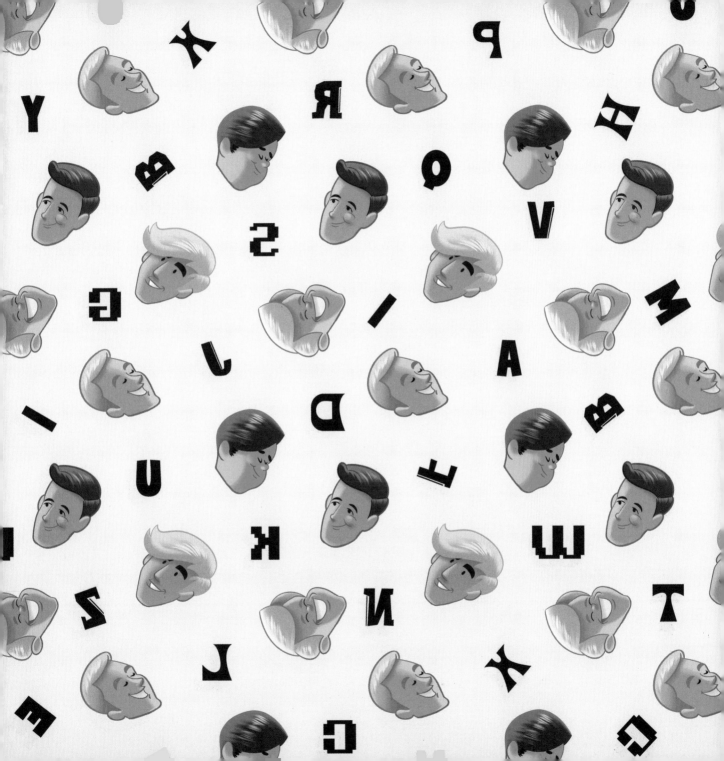

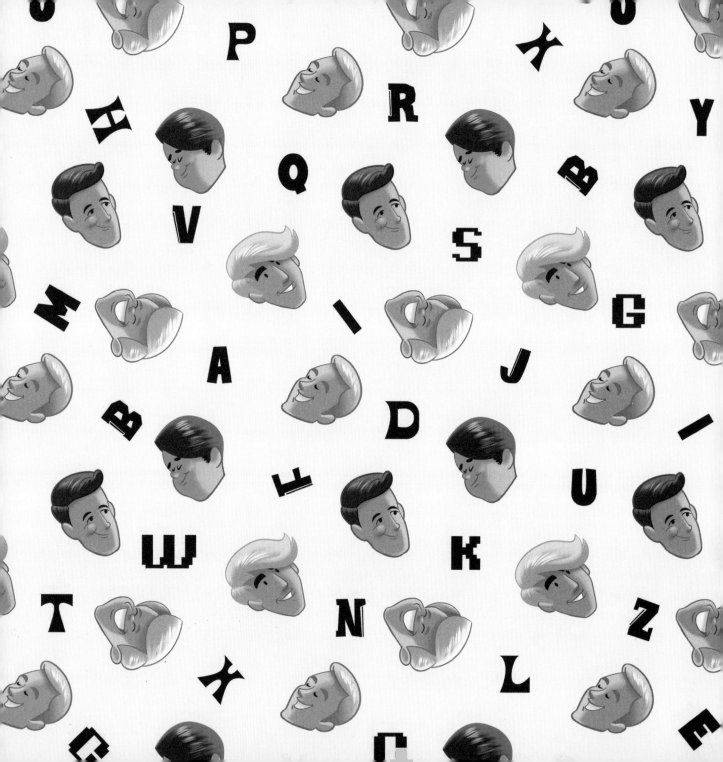